Tornadoes

CHRISTY STEELE

Nature on the Rampage

www.raintreepublishers.co.uk

Visit our website to find out more information about **Raintree** books.

To order:
- ☎ Phone 44 (0) 1865 888112
- 🖹 Send a fax to 44 (0) 1865 314091
- 🖳 Visit the Raintree Bookshop at www.raintreepublishers.co.uk to browse our catalogue and order online.

First published in Great Britain by Raintree Publishers, Halley Court, Jordan Hill, Oxford, OX2 8EJ, part of Harcourt Education.
Raintree is a registered trademark of Harcourt Education Ltd.

Consultant: Harold Brooks, Ph.D., National Severe Storms Laboratory, Norman, Oklahoma

Editorial: Isabel Thomas
Cover Design: Jo Sapwell and Michelle Lisseter
Production: Jonathan Smith

Originated by Dot Gradations
Printed and bound in China and Hong Kong by South China

ISBN 1 844 21221 1
07 06 05 04 03
10 9 8 7 6 5 4 3 2 1

British Library Cataloguing in Publication Data
Steele, Christy
Tornadoes. – (Nature on the Rampage)
1.Tornadoes – Juvenile literature
551.5'53
A catalogue for this book is available from the British Library

Acknowledgements
The publishers would like to thank the following for permission to reproduce photographs: Digital Stock, pp. **1, 4, 11, 12, 17, 20, 24, 26, 29.**

Cover photograph by Photodisc

Every effort has been made to contact copyright holders of any material reproduced in this book. Any omissions will be rectified in subsequent printing if notice is given to the publishers.

Contents

About tornadoes

A tornado is a spiral of fast, spinning wind. It is the strongest and most terrifying type of windstorm on the Earth. Its winds can blow at speeds of more than 480 kilometres (300 miles) per hour. The end of the spiral leaves a path of destruction where it touches the ground. The size of a tornado ranges from a few metres wide to over one kilometre (0.6 miles) wide, although tornadoes this large are very rare.

Tornadoes can strike at any time of year. In the USA, most tornadoes happen between March and August. About 1000 tornadoes hit the USA during this tornado season. In the UK, about 30 tornadoes are reported each year.

 This tornado in Kansas, USA, is just a few metres wide.

funnel cloud

dust envelope

debris cloud

A tornado begins

Most tornadoes start in **supercell** thunderstorms. Supercells have clouds more than 9.5 kilometres (6 miles) high. Heavy rain and **hailstones** can fall from these clouds. Hailstones are small chunks of ice that fall from the sky.

Supercells start when cold, dry air mixes with warm, moist air. Moist air has a lot of water in it. The water in the warm air cools as it rises. It falls back to the Earth as rain.

Tornadoes begin when warm air rises quickly and begins to spin. This can make a **funnel cloud**. A funnel cloud looks like a funnel. It is like a long upside-down cone, open at the bottom. A funnel cloud becomes a tornado if it reaches the ground. The winds in a tornado pick up dust, soil and **debris** from the ground. Debris can be anything from sand and parts of trees to cars.

Many tornadoes can grow from one supercell. Tornadoes often end when the supercell ends. A tornado can last from a few seconds to a few hours. Most tornadoes last less than 10 minutes.

◀ **This diagram shows the parts of a tornado.**

Where tornadoes happen

Tornadoes can happen anywhere in the world. India, Bangladesh and Australia have many tornadoes. In 1989, a tornado in Bangladesh killed about 1300 people.

Most tornadoes happen in the Great Plains of the USA. People call part of the Great Plains **Tornado Alley** because of the high number of tornadoes that happen there. The states in Tornado Alley are Nebraska, Kansas, Oklahoma and Texas.

In countries like the UK, the number of tornadoes each year changes. In most years, there are very few, but sometimes many strike at once. On 23 November 1981, 105 tornadoes were reported across the UK. Most UK tornadoes are small twisters and do very little damage.

How tornadoes move

Tornadoes move in different ways. Some tornadoes take straight paths. Some zigzag. Other tornadoes move in small circles on the ground. Tornadoes can grow bigger or smaller as they travel. In some places, a **damage path** may be just 1 kilometre (0.6 miles) wide. In other places, the same path may be 3 kilometres (2 miles) wide.

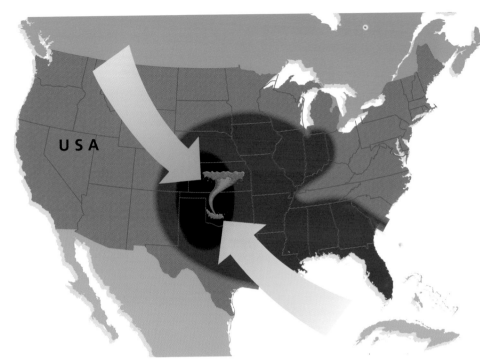

● high-risk tornado area   ➤ cool, dry air
● Tornado Alley   ➤ warm, moist air

▲ Warm, moist air and cold, dry air meet in Tornado Alley. The mixing air causes many tornadoes.

Meteorologists are scientists who study weather. They measure the size and wind speed of a tornado by the path of damage it leaves. Damage is harm or injury that causes loss or makes something less valuable.

Warning signs of a tornado
Tornadoes often start quickly. Watching the weather for signs of a tornado can give people time to reach a safe place.

- A funnel cloud may turn into a tornado.
- The sky may appear slightly green or green-black before a tornado.
- The air may become still just before a tornado.
- A strong thunderstorm that makes hail may also start a tornado.
- Noise may mean a tornado is near. A tornado's winds sound like a train or aeroplane.

A tornado's colour

A tornado's colour depends on the debris it carries. Tornadoes that carry mostly dust and soil are dark grey. Tornadoes carrying the coloured soil of the south-west USA look red-orange. Tornadoes above water are called **waterspouts**. Waterspouts pull water up into the funnel and look white or blue.

A tornado's colour also depends on the light. Tornadoes look white if the sun is shining on them. They look grey if they are in the shadow of the sun.

This tornado has sucked up soil from the field it ripped apart.

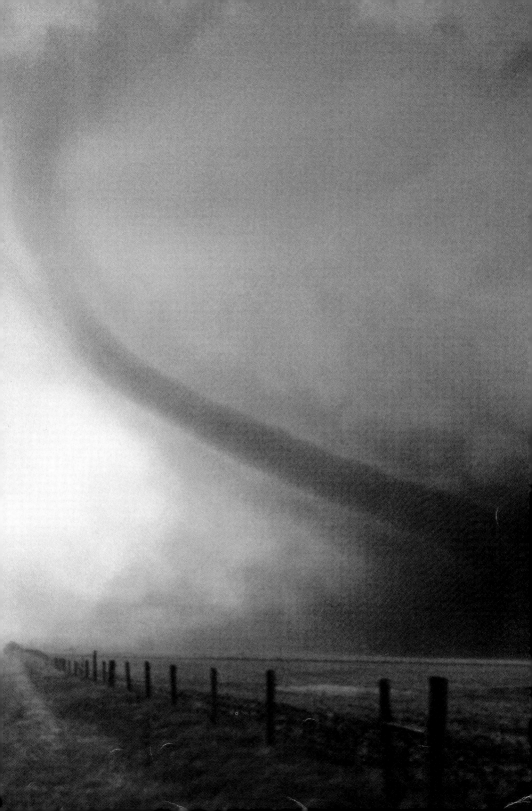

Killer tornadoes

Scientists in the early 1900s studied the weather to find out how tornadoes started. But they did not have all the right tools they needed to understand weather properly.

Without helpful tools and instruments, scientists could not warn people about tornadoes. To warn someone is to tell them that danger is coming. Tornadoes were more deadly in the past because people did not have time to get to a safe place.

Now there are better warnings and people know more about tornado safety, so the number of tornado deaths is falling. But tornadoes still kill over a hundred people every year.

 More than 40 people in the USA die in tornadoes each year.

Fujita-Pearson Tornado Scale

Scientists use the Fujita-Pearson Tornado Scale to rate how powerful tornadoes are. Scientists study the damage a tornado causes. They then give the tornado a number from F0 to F5. Powerful tornadoes receive higher numbers than weak tornadoes.

Most tornadoes are F0 or F1. These weak tornadoes do little damage. They may blow branches off trees. Only about one in a hundred tornadoes are F5. These killer tornadoes can blow down buildings and trees.

Some killer tornadoes

The most tornadoes to strike the USA in one day is about 150. This happened between 3 and 4 April, 1974. The tornadoes blew down every building in several towns. They smashed homes, schools and police stations. The tornadoes caused more than £366 million in damage. They killed 315 people.

In April 1998, powerful thunderstorms started a line of strong tornadoes in the USA. They ripped through three states, blowing down thousands of buildings. One of the tornadoes measured F5 on the Fujita-Pearson Scale and was the strongest to hit the state of Alabama for 20 years.

Fujita-Pearson Tornado Scale

F 5
Wind Speed: 420 to 512 km
(261 to 318 miles) per hour
Damage: Winds level everything in the tornado's path. The tornado lifts houses and smashes them to the ground. Vehicles fly through the air.

F 4
Wind Speed: 333 to 419 km
(207 to 260 miles) per hour
Damage: Winds blow down walls of buildings. The tornado lifts vehicles and debris. Winds uproot trees and break their trunks in half.

F 3
Wind Speed: 254 to 332 km
(158 to 206 miles) per hour
Damage: Winds tear off roofs. The tornado blows down trees and overturns cars.

F 2
Wind Speed: 182 to 253 km
(113 to 157 miles) per hour
Damage: Winds damage houses and trees.

F 1
Wind Speed: 117 to 181 km
(73 to 112 miles) per hour
Damage: Winds may damage roofs and signs.

F 0
Wind Speed: 64 to 116 km
(40 to 72 miles) per hour
Damage: Winds break tree branches.

Thirty-six people died and more than 273 were injured. Hundreds of millions of pounds worth of damage was done. But many people saved their lives by listening to tornado warnings and doing the right things to protect themselves. One family who lived in a mobile home ran down the street to take shelter in a friend's house. They survived, but their mobile home was completely destroyed.

May 1999 tornadoes

On 3 May 1999, several supercell storms blew into Oklahoma, in the USA. At least 70 strong tornadoes started in these storms and blew over three states.

Twenty-six of the tornadoes made damage paths through Oklahoma. Strong F4 tornadoes picked up cars and threw them into buildings. The tornadoes were the most costly in Oklahoma history. It cost more than £610 million to fix the tornado damage.

Meteorologists gave people warnings about the May tornadoes. The warnings saved many lives, but the tornadoes still killed 45 people. More than 670 people were hurt.

The Oklahoma tornadoes started in a supercell thunderstorm like this one.

Weird winds

A tornado's winds can do strange things. One tornado blew the walls of a building away. But it left shelves that leaned against the walls standing. Nothing even fell off the shelves. Another tornado pulled 16 students from their chairs and put them down 140 metres away. The students lived, but the tornado smashed the school.

Tornadoes can lift animals into the air. A French tornado once lifted the water, fish and frogs from a pond and dropped them many kilometres away. People thought it was raining fish and frogs.

One tornado lifted a herd of cows and sent them flying. They landed several kilometres away. Many of the cows lived. Another tornado blew the feathers off chickens. The chickens lived.

A tornado's winds can blow things so strongly that everyday objects become dangerous. One tornado blew a piece of plastic through a tree trunk. Tornado winds can make blades of grass and straw cut through wood and pieces of wood break through concrete. In 1992, an Australian F4 tornado had freak effects like jamming a picture frame into the wall of a room. Hailstones the size of cricket balls fell alongside the tornado.

Three deadly tornadoes in the USA

• Tri-State Tornado
On 18 March, 1925, a tornado touched down in Missouri. It was so low and wide that people could not see its funnel. It looked like a black cloud moving across the ground. The tornado travelled about 320 kilometres (200 miles) through Missouri, Illinois and Indiana.

The Tri-State Tornado was the worst tornado in history. It blew down every building in four towns. It killed about 700 people. Flying debris injured more than 2000 people.

• Natchez Tornado
On 7 May, 1840, a tornado touched down near Natchez, Mississippi. The tornado sucked up the trees along the banks of the Mississippi River. It also lifted rafts and steamboats off the river. It smashed them back into the water. Many boats sank and people drowned. The tornado killed 317 people. More than 100 people were hurt. This was the second worst tornado in USA history.

• St Louis Tornado
On 27 May, 1896, a tornado touched down in eastern St Louis, Missouri. The tornado was about 1.5 kilometres (1 mile) wide. It smashed houses, factories, hospitals and railway stations. About 255 people died in the St Louis Tornado. More than 1000 people were hurt. The death count makes it the third worst tornado in USA history.

Tornado safety

Meteorologists today use special tools to find out when tornadoes and other storms will strike. Meteorologists warn people when tornadoes might happen.

Meteorologists give a tornado watch during bad weather that may cause a tornado. This means that tornadoes might hit in the next few hours. People should listen to radio and television news during tornado watches. They should stay close to a safe place, like a strong building or cellar in case a tornado starts. People should also watch the sky for signs of a tornado.

 Some scientists now think that lightning can help them work out where tornadoes will start.

Tornado myths

Early people told stories called myths to explain the weather. In myths, powerful beings were said to be in charge of the weather.

• **In North America,** some American Indians believed that the Great Spirit sent tornadoes to punish people who did bad things. Other American Indians believed tornadoes destroyed old things so that new things could begin.

• **In Central America,** the Aztecs believed the wind god Ehécatl was in charge of the air. The Aztecs believed Ehécatl blew the Sun across the sky each day. They believed Ehécatl made tornadoes and other windstorms by blowing down on the Earth.

• **In Japan,** people believed the wind god Fujin controlled the air. They thought Fujin sent tornadoes and storms.

• **In India,** people believed that Indra was a god who made the weather. Indra sent tornadoes to hurt bad people.

Warnings and shelters

Meteorologists in tornado areas give a tornado warning if someone sees a tornado. Tornado sirens often sound during a tornado warning. People should treat tornado warnings seriously. They should go to a safe place straight away.

Tornado shelters are safe places to go during tornado warnings. These shelters are below ground. Tornadoes blow over the shelters and people inside stay safe. People can also take cover in the lowest level of a building. Cellars, rooms or cupboards without windows are the best places. People should protect themselves from flying debris by lying down and covering themselves with a blanket or mattress.

Never try to out-run a tornado. Do not try to watch or film a tornado. Never stay in a vehicle during a tornado. Leave the vehicle and find a strong building to shelter in, or find the nearest low part of dry ground such as a ditch and lie down in it. It is dangerous to hide under bridges or near trees as these often get destroyed by tornadoes. After the tornado has finished, people should stay away from broken electricity cables and damaged buildings, which could still collapse.

Being prepared

People living in high-risk tornado areas should keep a safety kit in the place where they shelter from tornadoes. The kit should contain a torch and a radio that runs on batteries, so they can listen to weather forecasts given on the radio. The kit should also include water, tinned food, blankets, medical supplies and extra batteries.

People should have tornado drills to practise what to do during a tornado. Offices and schools often have special drills, but families should have a plan too, in case a tornado strikes while they are at home. Everyone needs to learn the nearest safe place to go when a tornado hits. Someone should be in charge of bringing the tornado safety kit. People should also practise getting down low and covering their heads with their arms and hands to help protect themselves from flying debris.

◀ **A tornado lifted and dropped these cars.**

Tornadoes and science

Meteorologists still have questions about tornadoes. Scientists do not know how to predict what path a tornado will take. They do not know how big tornadoes will grow.

Meteorologists gather information about past tornadoes to answer these questions. They study what has happened before to help them find out when and where tornadoes begin. Scientists want to know how strong tornadoes will become.

◄ **This meteorologist is checking a weather map to look for storms.**

Storm chasers

Scientists need to see tornadoes up close to gather the best information. Some scientists do this by finding and chasing storms. An instrument called **Doppler radar** helps scientists find tornadoes. It measures wind speeds and rainfall. Scientists watch Doppler radar to find **supercells** that may create tornadoes.

Specially trained **volunteer** tornado spotters also help scientists find tornadoes. Volunteers are not paid for their help. Tornado spotters tell scientists about any tornadoes they see.

Storm chasers drive close to storms once they find them. They take pictures and videos of the storms. They study winds and damage paths.

The future of tornado science

Scientists have noticed that tornadoes often start under clouds where a lot of lightning flashes back and forth. People cannot see lightning that flashes between clouds so scientists use a new machine called an Optical Transient Detector (OTD) to find the lightning flashes. The OTD may help scientists predict when and where tornadoes will start.

▲ **This funnel cloud started in a supercell. It has turned into a weak tornado.**

Scientists are designing new machines that can be lifted by tornadoes without being damaged. These machines will send information back about what is happening inside the tornadoes.

Scientists hope that this new information will help them give earlier tornado warnings. Better warnings will help save people's lives.

Glossary

damage path area in which trees, buildings and other things are left damaged or destroyed by a tornado

debris (DEH-bree) flying objects carried by tornadoes

Doppler radar machine that measures wind speed and rainfall

funnel cloud cloud shaped like a funnel; a funnel cloud looks like an upside-down cone, open at the bottom

hailstone chunk of ice that falls from the sky during a storm

meteorologist scientist who studies weather

supercell (SOO-pur-cell) large, strong thunderstorm made up of huge clouds

Tornado Alley area in the USA that has lots of tornadoes every year

volunteer someone who does a job without pay

waterspout (WAH-tur-spowt) tornado that forms over water

Addresses and Internet sites

Met Office
London Road
Bracknell
Berkshire, RG12 2Z

Met Office
www.metoffice.gov.uk

BBC Weather Centre
www.bbc.co.uk/weather/weatherwise/factfiles/
extremes/tornadoes.shtml

Clouds R Us.com
www.rcn27.dial.pipex.com/cloudsrus/tornadoes.html

Commonwealth Bureau of Meteorology
www.bom.gov.au/lam/climate/levelthree/c20thc/
storm1.html

Australian Severe Weather
www.australiasevereweather.com

Index